Dedication

For Louisa and Russell

The Song of the Three-Pound Bug

By Rennick Steele

Design by Karen Morrison

"The Song of the Three-Pound Bug"

has been published thanks to a grant from

The Rockwell Foundation.

The Song of the Three-Pound Bug

I am a bug today,
Caught behind glass walls,
Enticed by a light,
Plainly visible beyond my reach.
Each time I fly toward it,
I find myself slapping up against the barrier.
There are those who say
That I would be happier to cease my buzzing
And that I should pass my time
Walking on the ceilings or munching
On some discarded apple core,
Both of which I like.
And I know that there is some truth to what they say,
For my wings ache so, and I grow tired of flying against
    the odds.
Often I wonder, "Are things meant to be this way?
Is it worth it after all, the light——?
I am only a bug."
But when I turn again to look,
I am enraptured by the halo's call,
And then I know I must do what I feel
Until my wings break.
Although I realize,
That even if there be a hole somewhere,
There is a great chance I may not fit.

Poem of the Morning Light

The things that really matter
Resolve into somebody soft and warm,
Someone with a genuine smile
Who laughs a lot,
An imperfection of the Universe,
Who's born lonely, cries, and needs to touch.
You and I can touch each other,
That's more than the sun can do to the moon.
So in the Light of spring,
Let the celebration of life,
The fire on the mountains awaken us,
And bring us down to daisies and bees.
For imperfection is soothed by awareness
Of you and me.
Lest we be like rocks on some moon,
Reflecting Light
As if Light meant nothing at all.

The Man Who Had Nothing to Do

To be mad
Is to be alone.
Hopelessly cut off,
Surrounded by blank space.
What do you do with blank space?
Find something or someone
To pass the time.
People have to be used.
You need a function.
A man without one
Went berserk on the subway yesterday.
He just sat there grinning
And grinding his teeth,
Screaming for someone
To sit with him.
The other passengers,
More embarrassed than afraid,
Just pretended he didn't exist.
And when the last stop came,
They left him there,
Screaming in an empty car,
Mad as a hatter
Alone as alone.

A Slice of Americana

Penny arcades are as American
As the Fourth of July.
"The soldiers lay dead in the rain.
Why don't they get up now?
I put my nickel in,
What's wrong, what's wrong?"
Penny arcades are everywhere,
They're not hard to find.
There's one right off Times Square.
Step right in...anything for sale—-
Madness for sale.
And you will see them practicing,
The children, that is.
Playing with clever machines
That kill mechanical men,
Who know when to get up
And when to fall down again.

It's only a game,
Something to occupy their time.
"We will let you play,"
The barkers there will say,
"Come one, come all!
Bring your nickels and your dimes,
And we will let you play.
Who we are never mind,
We will let you play."
Squeeze the triggers,
Push the buttons,
Pull the levers,
The numbers light up
To keep the score.
See the fascination in their eyes.
It's a bottom-line, red-blooded business,
There will always be penny arcades.
"The soldiers lay dead in the rain.
Why don't they get up now?
I put my nickel in,
What's wrong, what's wrong?"

The Simple Men*

Why is it always the simple man
Who must pay the price,
When the program calls for dying?
A simple man who rarely gets confused,
Enjoys a drink with friends,
The sight of mountains, the sound of seas,
The scent of a child's hair,
And before the day's work,
Coffee and the touch of a good woman's hand.
A simple man who doesn't want to control anyone,
Who just wants to live out his life in peace
    with those he loves,
Until his time is up.
Yet they come at him from every side
Screaming answers to questions
That only God can answer.
They speak of justice and freedom
As if it were as simple
As pulling a trigger.
And more often than not
It's a power play in the end,
Whoever wins.

And the new will have their day
As the old had theirs.
And when the killing's over
The old familiar faces will reappear
With different numbers on their backs,
And walk among the corpses
Of the simple men.

*For Graham Morgan, Retired Army Officer

David's Poem
or "Appearances"

This land has too much imperfection
And too much pain,
Where wide-eyed children starve,
And Angels die in the rain.
Come to a land of love and light.
Come out of the storm,
Come out of the night,
Come with me.
My land will not allow
The little ones to bleed
And the kind to die.
Come out of the storm,
Come out of the night,
Come with me.
We color the rainbow,
We blue the sky.
We are everywhere imagination can be.
We are old souls who pierce the night.
Come out of the darkness,
Come into the light,
You I love,
Come with me!

A Simple Reflex

It's just a matter
Of stimulus——response
A simple reflex,
You and I.
That's what they say.
And no one's responsible actually,
No one to set things right.
Right is relative, my friend.
Haven't you read B.F. Skinner?
So you can put your soliloquy away,
There's no need for it now.
Hamlets don't exist,
But homicide, ah homicide,
That's old hat!
It's just a matter
Of stimulus——response.
You know the Crypts shot a mailman today,
No reasons given, no questions asked.
They just opened up on the unsuspecting fellow.
Now who's to blame?
It's just a matter
Of stimulus——response.
But don't worry,
The sirens will take care of everything.
Besides, I'm sure we'll get to see it,
Close-up with Dan Rather
Tonight on the Evening News.

On Seeing an Old Photograph of a Pretty Young Girl

Caught unaware in the photograph of a moment,
You stand forever pretty in your static world,
Staring out of a time long since scattered by change.
When I look in your eyes I often wonder,
What the sound of your voice was like,
How warm your laughter was,
How soft your hands,
How silken your feet,
And what thought was buzzing through your brain,
Just at the instant the shutter closed,
And plucked you candidly out of time.
That will always remain a mystery to me,
Always a mystery to me.

Burned Out

You probably don't remember me,
But I'm the man in the moon.
I hope you don't mind
If I sit on your hill
And talk with you awhile.
You see of late I've noticed
That you seem to be changing,
Growing very hard,
Guarding against emotion
As if it were some hindrance
Like perspiration or dying.
There you sit
In your well-lit, rosy-glass jar,
Pretending to be content with
Staring at your fish bowl.
You say you're done
With stepping in front of trains,
And you've got to be on top from now on,
In control with no strings attached.
And that is so very sad to me,
For you will not let yourself
Be vulnerable anymore,
And vulnerable you must be
To get into heaven.

To a Scarlet Tomorrow

Why do we complicate
Such a simple thing as you and me,
As simple as a touch of soft hair
On a bare shoulder.
There's nothing contrived
About your eyes in the morning sun,
And once when I aligned
The stars for you
With my mind,
You knew,
That all along I chose to care.
When you're sad,
And alone with fear,
Know, know
That just beyond the moon
Somewhere, somewhere
I'll care, I'll care.

To Mary

Are you so incomprehensible
That I cannot hope to understand how you feel?
Can nothing bridge the gap between our minds?
I see in the windows of your eyes
The pain of being confined in a time
And a place——alone.
But you mustn't look too long at suns
For they will only make you blind.
Don't ask why or how, just dance.
Dance and laugh and be drunk
With spinning and remember this——
If I get lost in some moment,
Or if in the swirling blur of your dance
Our eyes don't meet again.
When I am dreams away from here
And my thoughts turn to the West,
I'll smile and remember you.

The Girl from Beyond the Tracks

Do I dare get off the train,
Carrying me to that leaden solitude,
Or shall I sit here
And let the world pass by in a blur?
Changes keep flashing before me,
Lights, sounds, and faces of holiday friends,
Confusing me even more than I am.
At the last stop,
I saw a town with a pretty girl.
She was standing in a meadow beyond the tracks.
Her back was turned, but it seemed as though,
Just for an instant, she turned her head
And caught my gaze in hers.
Then the great engine began to turn its wheels.
Without volition but more from habit,
And we were in motion as before.
I turned again to look,
But she was buried in the distance.
I thought of getting off at the next stop,
But that would be complicated,
Since I don't know how to unfold.
Besides, it's only nine minutes and thirty-two seconds
To supper.

Innocence

The Big They,
They say
That a man loses
His innocence
When he lays
For the first time
In bed with a woman.
I disagree.
A man loses his innocence
If he comes to believe
That he is nothing special.
He's not a hero now
And will never be.

New York, New York

Brave city of glass and steel
And sweat and blood.
And wonderful souls.
Key to the continent,
A nation's cauldron of all her people.
Town where I met my love, Marushka,
At the Cusack's apartment.
It was a Labor Day picnic.
Then, five years later we fell in love
Playing lovers at the Cusack's theatre.
We got married at the Churchill,
In Miss Rabitsch's apartment,
With the Twin Towers majestic in the sun
Behind us as a back drop,
Reminding us that wherever we go,
Whatever we do,
Whatever we become,
New York has shaped us.
We are forever New Yorkers.
Today when I contemplate the horror
Of the destruction of the World Trade Center,
I think of the brave firemen, medics and policemen,
Rushing upward past the stream of frightened
    office workers,
Not thinking of themselves, but of saving people's lives,
That's their job -
That's what they get paid for -
Without question,
That's what they live and die for.
They're the world's finest,
They're New Yorkers!

The Day
the Dolphins Came

The dolphins,
As if resigned to madness,
Swam hell-bent for the shore,
And beat their heads, bloody,
Against the rocks,
To languish in the killing air
Beached under a hot, seemingly indifferent sun.
What did they hope to find
From the mammals of the land?
If only we could speak to dolphins
The people said,
Then we could ask them why?
And why was all they said.
And the dolphins lay dead,
The dolphins lay dead.

Advice to Old Men

When the time comes,
All old men should put out to sea.
For the poets say that all men are sailors,
Caught out of water,
Forever looking down to the sea
From whence they came.
So old men,
While the tide is high,
And the wind is still fair,
Sail out,
Far from the land,
Out where the storms
Can cut you clean.
One last reckoning
Between two old friends.
No bedsores or boredom out there,
Oh, no,
Just your mind in time
With the water and the sun.
And then the sea will take old men
Back to mystery.

Hollywood

Factory of dreams,
Place of nightmares.
Life is not a track meet.
The brightest and the best
Are ground up like hamburger here.
So you've written one good play?
I've written fifty.
Give me this one play, and I'll produce your next.
You'll be rich and famous.
"But you didn't write the play."
What does that matter?
What are you, a wise guy or something?
You've got to play ball kid.
If you don't, well then
We can arrange for you to fall off a bridge to nowhere.
The door to Hollywood only opens once,
And when it shuts, it shuts damn hard!
"But you didn't write the play."
What does that matter.
Good artists borrow, great artists steal.
Besides, who's picking your wife up from work tonight?
How'd you like some water in your brake lines?
It's nothing personal, it's just business
You understand.

Hey, We're Just Trying to Take You Home!

Driving a yellow taxi
In the Big Apple
Was one interesting experience.
We were a strange lot,
Mostly immigrants, artists, and crazies.
It was mainly the money.
Quick cash in the hand is worth two in the bush.
Just don't pick up any fares
Out on Bushwhack Avenue late at night in the rain
When you can't see very well.
Hey, we're just trying to take you home!
Twenty shot dead and eighty wounded
Mostly crippled, shots to the head.
But '82 was a good year.
It's worse now.
To do it right you've got to become part of the cab.
Like a sparkplug or a radiator cap.
Then you don't feel anything.
You're a replaceable part.
Twelve hour shifts, seven days a week,
Five in the afternoon until five in the morning.
There's beauty out there though,
On a cool, crisp winter night
Coming up over the Queensborough Bridge
With Manhattan lit up like a diamond tiara.

Beautiful women getting into your cab in nylons
      and evening gowns,
Driving them through steam clouds
Rising up from under the streets
Depositing them at doorman-guarded buildings.
But don't look too long
Because around the next block
It's Terry and the Pirates,
And junkies, pimps, whores, and
Ex-cons looking for a quick grubstake.
Waiting for $200 bucks to roll by.
Back at the garage we talk.
Mitch the opera man sings out,
"I never met a cabby
That wasn't robbed at least once."
I tell him I got into a tight spot at Penn Station.
Jumped by three punks,
Fists flew, blood did too.
I yell out for cops, but no one hears,
At crowded Penn Station no less,
Except Yonni, the skinny Israeli kid from my garage,
Who dodges between the screeching cars,
And together we go about saving my life.

Dayton, Pennsylvania

Coming to school on a crisp, fall morning,
It's dark outside when I begin my journey.
I drive toward the rising sun,
Spectacular orange light rays shine
Off purple clouds that herald the morning's arrival.
Light fog and mist hover over the fields
As I make my turn on Route 839
And drive north toward Dayton.
Dayton, a farming town of simple, subtle beauty,
Where Americans have lived for generations,
Peopled by heroic folk who founded the Republic,
Fought and bled in all her wars,
Farmed the land, worked the mines and the factories,
Gentle folks with gentle hearts,
Who are proud of their rock-solid community.
It's a place where the good kids strive for excellence,
And the bad kids are still good at heart.
I pass the grand old oak tree just south of town
Whose arms seem to hold up the sky.
Soon, I'm in the parking lot and Mr. Cribbs
Greets me with a hearty smile.
I walk into the school and down the hall,
Everything seems at once old and new,
The blending of past and present.
I think for a moment,
"I wish all students could go to a school like Dayton High.
This is the way it used to be when I was a kid."
I wonder if our present students will look back
Twenty years from now and realize what a special place
Dayton High School really is?

Ursa Major and Ursa Minor

Hug-a-bears
Travel in pairs,
Are exceedingly rare,
Try to be fair,
Often dare,
Are beyond compare,
Live in a lair,
Try not to err,
Never despair,
Always care,
Just love Fred Astair.
The Hug-a-bears
Live in a magical forest
And occasionally scamper out into the world,
To surprise people
And then they run back inside to hide together.

Becki

Polish-American father-in-law
Raised up on the Depression streets of Detroit.
Lost his beautiful, musical mother, Edna-Estelle,
    at fourteen.
She imbued in him a love for music, and then she died.
He learned to play a honey sounding horn,
Made ten times what his step-dad made in the shop
Playing in blind pigs,
Johnny and his horn.
Pearl Harbor changes everything,
Drafted into the service,
Maybe play in the band?
Too much rhythm,
Assigned to radio school going to be a flyboy.
Flies the heavy's on practice missions out
    over the Rockies,
Saved a plane once lost in a storm.
Brought it down with just his jazz ears
Between two mountains in Salt Lake City,
Fire pots lining the runway.

Soon it's off to the war with Captain Slayton
    in "Little Lambsy Divey."
Arrive in Norwich in early forty-four.
At Horsham St. Faiths with the 458th.
First one is Berlin and a rough one,
Flight suit short circuit,
Stay in the turret too many Messerschmitts coming in,
Chosen to be frozen
Grounded for four weeks.
Time to unthaw with a trip to London
To dance with the English girls,
Then back to Horsham St. Faiths to dance with
    the Jerries,
Thirty-one missions over the Reich.
D-Day and the crew sings Happy Birthday to Becki
Over the intercom.
Soon it's V-E Day, and it's back to the States.
Got to find a jazz girl and start a family,
Alex comes singing into his life,
Helps him through the "shakes."
They get married and have Marushka and Jad.
Big bands are dead, so it's time to learn tool and dye,
To put bread on the table.
Working in a shop as your step-dad did,
Providing for your family.
Air Force doctors say you got a problem Sergeant Becki,
Gotta drink red wine for your frozen veins for
    the rest of your life.
Can do, Sir, can do!
So you learn to make it with Mr. Larco in the basement,
Then Jonathan and Alex, Jad and Maru lived
Happily forever after.

Daddy

Jonathan, Jonathan
Orange hat rat-a-tat-tat!
The birds and the squirrels
In your care.
You sensed deeply
The despair, despair
Seeking the same sense of you
In the Air.
Your natural habitat of life.
And oh, Jonathan!
You brought such intensity and feeling
To the wide spaces of your life.
You gave such intensity and feeling
To the spaces of my life——
Do you hear the birds?
Can you hear my cries
In the middle of the night
Praying for a sign
That you have landed safely?
The birds sing Taps and fly
As though they are winging their way to Normandy.
Reminding my grateful heart
Of life's great sacrifices.

Soar birds——
Are you looking for Jonathan
Of the orange hat?
His pockets laden with tasty nuts
To place gently in the tree with the hole.
Oh Daddy, how you loved all living creatures.
How I loved to sit in your lap when I arrived home
From the far reaches of the world,
And know that I was Daddy's girl.
When I look up some nights,
I can feel your life vibrating in chromatic scales
Of clear trumpet notes,
Rat-a-tat-tat,
In the star-laden vastness of heaven.

By Marushka Steele

Alex

Eighth Air Force girl,
Jazz baby with style,
Marushka's mother, Alex
Comes to reside at Wild Thyme.
She brings with her
The flamenco dancer on the wall
And the lone Indian above the fireplace
And her beautiful soul.
She is here to help
The hug-a-bears organize their lives,
And to take care of the cats
And make sure the goat gets fed
And the roses bloom.
What an honor it is to have her here
After Jonathan's last flight west.

Uncle Jack

My Indian uncle,
Was at heart a kid,
Like us.
He looked like a dark Dana Andrews
    and talked like Randolph Scott.
He used to climb the hill with us cousins
When the snow was deep
And ride the toboggan
Down toward the creek
At fifty miles an hour,
Then bail out with the rest of us,
Before we hit the bottom
And hope not to land
On a frozen cow turd
Hidden in the snow.
He was an Eagle Scout without a dad,
The first to be drafted,
So he joined the Marines and
Got to see exotic places like
Bougainville and Iwo Jima.
He was my warrior uncle,
At the point of Uncle Sam's spear,
And he never talked about it,
Except to himself late at night
In his nightmares.

The Farm

Young Navy Lieutenant in starched whites,
Meets a young Cherokee lady from Oklahoma
On scholarship north to P.C.W.
They fall in love and get married.
Then he is off to the South Pacific
Putting bombs and depth charges on Venturas
While she finishes her nurse's training.
When John returns
They move to his boyhood dream,
The farm.
Three kids come in quick succession:
Ellen, Ren, and Charlie,
They hack it out farming for fifteen years.

Times change, economic hardships.
Jeannie goes back to work
As the nurse she was trained to be,
Papa John helps build roads
And is transferred to Ohio.
We leave the farm
And for twenty years
Travel the earth.
Then we all come back one day,
Paint the old barn,
Build up the ruined fences,
And buy a horse, a sheep, and a goat.
Fire up the H
And start making hay,
Again.

An American Family

We drive six hours southeast
To Annapolis, an old Navy town
Where my Aunt Wanda lives,
Cherokee beauty – Navy widow.
She remains at her last posting
Near the Academy's Main Gate.
We come to celebrate Sarah and Frank's marriage.
They have lasted twenty years with
    two beautiful children
One of each kind.
It is a happy, joyous occasion,
As I look around the room filled with cousins
    and relatives,
And good friends.
Mostly Christians with a sprinkling of Hebrews,
Mostly brunettes, some blondes
Some blue eyes, some brown, some black, some green,
Some dark, some light, some in between.
Everyone is laughing and talking,
Papa John winks and whispers
That he forgot the old goat, Hans.
He was going to bring him down from the farm,
For the Middies to take care of.
Everyone laughs, and we sing away into the night.

Freeport, Pennsylvania-
My Hometown

Freeport, pearl along the Allegheny,
The river the Indians called the Beautiful River,
Old settler's town,
Massey Harbison's children –
The blood consecrated ground.
Natives and Europeans
Once hated each other,
Now forever mixed
Into Heinz Fifty-seven Varieties.
Catholics and Protestants and Jews all mixed
Together.
Makes the blood stronger,
Better that way.
Freeport, the old canal boat and railroad town.
John Shoup's store still on Market Street.
I can still see my Great-great-great
Grandfather's footsteps in the frosty grass
By the riverside.

Rose of Sharon

May you always
Have a rose in your springs,
And old friends in winter
To mend broken wings.